Contents

Introduction

Buddhism is a spiritual and philosophical tradition that began over 2,500 years ago in South Asia. It developed from the teachings attributed to Gautama Buddha and later spread across large parts of Asia and, eventually, the world. As Buddhism moved through different cultures, it adapted to local languages, customs, and artistic traditions, giving rise to a wide range of practices and interpretations.

Despite this diversity, Buddhist traditions share a common focus on understanding suffering and the conditions that give rise to it. Buddhist teachings explore how ignorance, attachment, and misunderstanding shape human experience. Through awareness, ethical conduct, and reflection, Buddhism offers ways to reduce suffering and cultivate clarity, compassion, and balance.

Buddhism does not center on belief in a single creator deity. Instead, it emphasizes observation, experience, and insight. Many Buddhist teachings encourage individuals to examine their own thoughts and actions, recognizing how choices influence both personal wellbeing and the lives of others. This approach has allowed Buddhism to develop in many forms while maintaining shared core principles.

As Buddhism spread to regions such as India, Sri Lanka, Tibet, Nepal, China, Korea, Japan, and Southeast Asia, it absorbed local symbols, stories, and artistic styles. These regional influences shaped how teachings were expressed, leading to a rich variety of texts, rituals, images, and symbolic figures. Some of these figures are historical, while others represent key ideas or qualities.

The figures presented in this book are part of this symbolic and cultural landscape. They are not creator gods, but figures who serve specific roles within Buddhist traditions. Some represent complete awakening, while others embody compassion, wisdom, protection, or ethical responsibility. Their forms and meanings may differ across regions, reflecting the diversity of Buddhist cultures.

Buddhism organizes these figures into categories based on their roles and functions. These categories help explain how different figures relate to Buddhist teachings and practices. Understanding these groupings makes it easier to see how ideas such as awakening, compassion, protection, and moral responsibility are expressed in visual and narrative form.

Because Buddhism is practiced in many cultures, no single explanation can represent all interpretations. The descriptions in this book reflect commonly shared understandings found across traditions, while acknowledging regional differences. This approach allows readers to appreciate both the unity and diversity within Buddhism.

Together, the figures and categories in this book offer insight into how Buddhist traditions explore the human experience. Through symbols, stories, and teachings, Buddhism presents ways of understanding suffering, cultivating wisdom, and acting with care toward others. This introduction provides a foundation for exploring the many figures that follow and the ideas they represent.

Buddhas

Buddhas are fully awakened beings who have reached complete enlightenment. They have gained deep understanding of reality and teach paths that help others reduce suffering and develop wisdom. Some Buddhas are historical figures, while others are described in later Buddhist traditions. Across cultures, Buddhas represent clarity, insight, and awakening.

Amitābha

Amitābha is known as the Buddha of Infinite Light and Infinite Life. He is one of the most widely recognized Buddhas in Buddhism and appears in many traditions across Asia. Amitābha is especially important in Mahayana Buddhism, including traditions found in Tibet, Mongolia, Nepal, China, Korea, Japan, and parts of India. His name is associated with boundless light, compassion, and clarity.

In many Buddhist texts, Amitābha is connected with the concept of the Pure Land, often called Sukhāvatī. The Pure Land is described as a realm created through Amitābha's vows, where conditions are especially supportive for spiritual learning. While interpretations differ among Buddhist schools, the Pure Land is generally understood as a place representing peace, understanding, and freedom from suffering and confusion.

Amitābha is commonly shown seated in meditation, holding a bowl that symbolizes generosity and care for all beings. In Buddhist art, he is often depicted with red or golden coloring, representing warmth, wisdom, and illuminating awareness. In Tibetan Buddhism, Amitābha is also associated with meditation practices that cultivate compassion and insight, while in East Asian traditions he plays a central role in devotional and contemplative practices.

Across the many cultures where Amitābha is known, he represents the idea that awakening is supported by compassion and understanding. His presence in Buddhist traditions reflects a shared emphasis on patience, kindness, and the possibility of growth, even in difficult circumstances. Though practices and interpretations vary by region, Amitābha remains a unifying figure whose symbolism points toward clarity, care, and the easing of suffering.

Bhaiṣajyaguru

Bhaiṣajyaguru is known as the Medicine Buddha, a figure associated with healing, wellbeing, and the relief of suffering. He appears in several branches of Mahayana Buddhism and is especially important in Tibetan, Chinese, Korean, Japanese, and Himalayan Buddhist traditions. His name is often connected with medicine, care, and the restoration of balance in both body and mind.

In Buddhist texts, Bhaiṣajyaguru is described as a Buddha who made vows to help beings overcome illness, pain, and hardship. These teachings emphasize that suffering can arise from both physical conditions and mental distress. Across traditions, Bhaiṣajyaguru is understood as representing the idea that healing involves wisdom, ethical living, and compassion, not only medical treatment.

Bhaiṣajyaguru is commonly depicted seated in meditation, holding a bowl of medicine or a healing plant. In Buddhist art, his body is often shown in deep blue, symbolizing calmness, clarity, and the healing power of awareness. In Tibetan Buddhism, he is closely associated with healing rituals and meditation practices, while in East Asian traditions he is frequently invoked in prayers related to health, protection, and recovery.

Across the regions where Bhaiṣajyaguru is honored, he represents the principle that care and understanding play a central role in wellbeing. Although practices and interpretations vary by culture, his symbolism consistently points toward compassion, balance, and the possibility of healing through mindful and caring action.

Gautama Buddha

Gautama Buddha, also known as Śākyamuni Buddha, was the historical teacher whose life and teachings gave rise to Buddhism. He lived in northern India around the 5th century BCE and is regarded across all Buddhist traditions as the awakened teacher who discovered a path to understanding suffering and its causes. His life story forms the shared foundation of Buddhism in South Asia, East Asia, and Southeast Asia.

According to Buddhist texts, Gautama Buddha taught that suffering arises from craving, misunderstanding, and attachment. He introduced the Middle Way, a path that avoids extremes and emphasizes balance, ethical conduct, meditation, and insight. While different Buddhist traditions emphasize various aspects of his teachings, his core message of awareness, compassion, and responsibility remains central across cultures.

Gautama Buddha is commonly shown seated in meditation, symbolizing stillness, focus, and clarity. In early Indian and Theravāda traditions found in Sri Lanka, Thailand, Myanmar, Cambodia, and Laos, he is often emphasized as a historical teacher whose teachings are preserved in monastic practice and scripture. In Mahayana and Vajrayana traditions, his role is sometimes understood alongside cosmic Buddhas and Bodhisattvas, while still honoring him as the original teacher of the Dharma.

Across regions and centuries, Gautama Buddha represents the possibility of awakening through understanding and practice. Although Buddhist traditions have developed in diverse ways, his life and teachings continue to guide reflection on suffering, compassion, and the cultivation of wisdom. His presence in Buddhist cultures around the world reflects a shared commitment to mindful living and ethical awareness.

Bodhisattvas

Bodhisattvas are enlightened beings dedicated to helping others. Rather than seeking final liberation only for themselves, they remain engaged with the world to support those who suffer. Bodhisattvas represent compassion, wisdom, patience, and ethical action. Their forms and stories vary widely across Buddhist traditions.

Mañjuśrī

Mañjuśrī is known as the Bodhisattva of Wisdom and is one of the most important figures in Mahayana Buddhism. He appears prominently in Buddhist traditions across India, Tibet, Nepal, China, Korea, and Japan, where he represents insight, understanding, and the clarity that comes from deep awareness. His name is closely associated with the development of wisdom through study, reflection, and practice.

In Buddhist teachings, Mañjuśrī embodies the idea that wisdom arises from recognizing the true nature of reality. He is strongly connected with teachings on emptiness, insight, and discernment found in Mahayana scriptures. While different traditions emphasize different texts and practices, Mañjuśrī is consistently understood as guiding beings beyond confusion and misunderstanding toward clear seeing.

Mañjuśrī is commonly depicted holding a flaming sword and a book of teachings. The sword symbolizes the ability to cut through ignorance and mistaken views, while the book represents knowledge, learning, and the transmission of insight. In Tibetan Buddhism, Mañjuśrī is often associated with scholarly study and meditation practices, while in East Asian traditions he is closely linked with monastic education and the cultivation of understanding.

Across the many regions where Mañjuśrī is honored, he represents the principle that wisdom must be cultivated carefully and responsibly. Although practices and interpretations vary among Buddhist cultures, his symbolism consistently points toward thoughtful inquiry, clarity of mind, and the importance of understanding as a foundation for compassionate action.

Avalokiteśvara

Avalokiteśvara is known as the Bodhisattva of Compassion and is one of the most widely recognized figures in Mahayana Buddhism. He appears in Buddhist traditions across India, Tibet, Nepal, China, Korea, Japan, and Southeast Asia, where he represents empathy, care for suffering beings, and the commitment to respond to the needs of others. His name is often understood as "the one who observes the cries of the world."

In Buddhist texts and teachings, Avalokiteśvara embodies the idea that compassion is an active response to suffering. He is described as remaining closely connected to the world in order to help beings who are experiencing fear, pain, or confusion. While interpretations vary among traditions, Avalokiteśvara is consistently associated with the intention to ease suffering through understanding and kindness.

Avalokiteśvara is depicted in many different forms across regions. In Tibetan Buddhism, he is known as Chenrezig and is often shown with many arms and eyes, symbolizing the ability to see suffering everywhere and to respond in countless ways. In East Asian traditions, he is commonly known as Guanyin in China and Kannon in Japan, where his imagery often emphasizes gentleness, mercy, and attentive care.

Across the cultures where Avalokiteśvara is honored, he represents the principle that compassion is central to Buddhist practice. Although artistic forms, names, and practices differ by region, his symbolism consistently points toward listening, understanding, and responding thoughtfully to the suffering of others. His presence in Buddhist traditions highlights the shared importance of compassion as a guiding force in human life.

Kṣitigarbha

Kṣitigarbha is known as a Bodhisattva associated with compassion for beings who suffer, particularly those in difficult or transitional states of existence. He is an important figure in Mahayana Buddhism and is especially prominent in East Asian traditions, including China, Korea, and Japan, while also appearing in Tibetan and Indian sources. His name is often interpreted as "Earth Treasury," symbolizing steadiness, patience, and deep compassion.

In Buddhist teachings, Kṣitigarbha is associated with a vow to assist beings who experience intense suffering, including those described in hell realms or states of deep distress. These descriptions are understood differently across traditions. In many contexts, they are seen not only as literal realms, but also as symbolic expressions of suffering, fear, and confusion. Kṣitigarbha represents the commitment to care for beings who are most in need of support.

Kṣitigarbha is commonly depicted as a monk holding a staff and a jewel. The staff symbolizes guidance and protection, while the jewel represents clarity, hope, and the ability to bring light into dark or difficult situations. In Japan, where he is known as Jizō, Kṣitigarbha is closely associated with caring for children, travelers, and those in vulnerable conditions. In Chinese Buddhism, he is often linked with rituals and teachings focused on compassion and remembrance.

Across the regions where Kṣitigarbha is honored, he represents the principle that compassion does not turn away from suffering. Although cultural interpretations and practices vary, his symbolism consistently points toward patience, responsibility, and the willingness to help others through difficult circumstances. His presence in Buddhist traditions highlights the importance of care, guidance, and compassion directed toward those who are often overlooked.

Vajrapāṇi

Vajrapāṇi is known as a Bodhisattva associated with strength, protection, and spiritual power. He appears in Buddhist traditions across India, Tibet, Nepal, Central Asia, China, and Japan, where he represents the force needed to defend wisdom and compassion. His name means "Holder of the Vajra," referring to the thunderbolt symbol that represents indestructible clarity and energy.

In Buddhist teachings, Vajrapāṇi embodies the active power that supports awakening. While some Bodhisattvas emphasize compassion or wisdom, Vajrapāṇi is associated with the strength required to overcome obstacles such as fear, confusion, and harmful actions. Across traditions, he is understood not as a figure of aggression, but as one who protects the path of understanding and guards the teachings from distortion.

Vajrapāṇi is often depicted in a powerful stance, holding a vajra and sometimes shown with a fierce expression. This imagery is symbolic rather than threatening. In Tibetan Buddhism, Vajrapāṇi is closely associated with protective rituals and meditation practices that cultivate inner strength and resilience. In East Asian traditions, he appears as a guardian figure often placed at temple entrances, representing protection and alertness.

Across the regions where Vajrapāṇi is known, he represents the principle that compassion and wisdom sometimes require strength to be upheld. Although artistic styles and ritual roles vary by culture, his symbolism consistently points toward courage, stability, and the energy needed to protect what is beneficial. His presence in Buddhist traditions highlights the role of strength when guided by understanding and ethical intention.

Prajñāpāramitā

Prajñāpāramitā is associated with transcendent wisdom in Mahayana Buddhism and represents the deep understanding that goes beyond ordinary concepts and distinctions. Her name means "Perfection of Wisdom," referring both to a central Buddhist teaching and to a symbolic figure that embodies this insight. Prajñāpāramitā appears in Buddhist traditions across India, Tibet, Nepal, China, Korea, and Japan, primarily through philosophical texts, art, and ritual symbolism.

In Buddhist teachings, Prajñāpāramitā is closely connected with scriptures that explore the nature of reality, emptiness, and insight. These teachings emphasize that wisdom arises from seeing things as they truly are, without attachment to fixed ideas. Across traditions, Prajñāpāramitā is understood less as a historical being and more as a representation of awakened understanding itself.

Prajñāpāramitā is often depicted in human form holding a book or manuscript, symbolizing the transmission of wisdom teachings. In Tibetan and Himalayan art, she may appear as a calm, luminous figure representing insight and clarity. In East Asian traditions, the concept of Prajñāpāramitā is more often emphasized through study, recitation, and philosophical reflection rather than visual representation.

Across the regions where Prajñāpāramitā is known, she represents the principle that wisdom is essential to liberation from suffering. Although cultural expressions and artistic forms differ, her symbolism consistently points toward clarity, discernment, and insight into the nature of experience. Her presence in Buddhist traditions highlights the importance of understanding as a foundation for compassion and ethical action.

Tārā

Bodhisattvas

Tārā Bodhisattvas are manifestations of compassion and swift aid. They are especially important in Vajrayana and Himalayan Buddhist traditions. Tārā figures emphasize responsiveness, protection, healing, and care, highlighting compassion expressed through immediate and practical action.

Green Tārā

Green Tārā is known as a Bodhisattva associated with compassion in action, especially the swift response to fear, danger, and suffering. She is a prominent figure in Mahayana and Vajrayana Buddhism, particularly in Tibet, Nepal, Bhutan, Mongolia, and Himalayan regions, and is also known in parts of India and East Asia. Green Tārā represents active care, readiness to help, and the immediate application of compassion.

In Buddhist traditions, Green Tārā is understood as a figure who responds quickly to the needs of others. She is associated with protection from fear and obstacles, both external and internal. While stories and practices related to Green Tārā vary across regions, she is consistently linked with the idea that compassion should be responsive, attentive, and engaged rather than distant or passive.

Green Tārā is commonly depicted seated with one leg extended, symbolizing readiness to rise and act. Her green color represents growth, vitality, and active energy. In Tibetan Buddhism, Green Tārā is closely associated with meditation practices and chants focused on courage and compassionate response. In other traditions, she appears primarily as a symbol of reassurance, protection, and care.

Across the regions where Green Tārā is honored, she represents the principle that compassion can be immediate and effective. Although artistic styles, rituals, and interpretations differ among cultures, her symbolism consistently points toward responsiveness, courage, and the willingness to help when help is needed. Her presence in Buddhist traditions highlights the importance of acting with care and awareness in moments of difficulty.

White Tārā

White Tārā is known as a Bodhisattva associated with longevity, healing, and compassionate care. She appears primarily in Vajrayana Buddhism, especially in Tibet, Nepal, Bhutan, Mongolia, and Himalayan regions, and is also known in parts of India and East Asia. White Tārā represents calm compassion, patience, and the nurturing aspects of wisdom.

In Buddhist traditions, White Tārā is connected with the preservation of life and the easing of physical and mental suffering. She is often associated with practices related to health, recovery, and long life. While interpretations and practices differ across regions, White Tārā is consistently understood as symbolizing gentle care, stability, and sustained wellbeing rather than immediate or forceful action.

White Tārā is commonly depicted seated in meditation, often with seven eyes located on her face, hands, and feet. These eyes symbolize awareness that sees suffering clearly and responds with understanding. Her white color represents purity, clarity, and peaceful healing. In Tibetan Buddhism, she is closely associated with meditation and ritual practices focused on longevity and calm awareness.

Across the regions where White Tārā is honored, she represents the principle that compassion can be steady, patient, and sustaining. Although artistic styles, texts, and practices vary among cultures, her symbolism consistently points toward care that supports life over time, balance in body and mind, and the quiet strength of attentive compassion. Her presence in Buddhist traditions highlights the value of nurturing wellbeing through wisdom and mindful action.

Protective Deities

(Dharmapālas)

Protective deities, also known as Dharmapālas, are fierce guardians of wisdom and compassion. Their strong appearance is symbolic, representing decisiveness, strength, and the removal of obstacles. They protect the teachings of Buddhism and support ethical conduct, clarity, and awareness rather than aggression or harm.

Mahākāla

Mahākāla is known as a protective figure associated with the safeguarding of Buddhist teachings. He appears primarily in Vajrayana Buddhism, especially in Tibet, Nepal, Bhutan, Mongolia, and Himalayan regions, and has historical roots in Indian Buddhist traditions. Mahākāla represents vigilance, protective strength, and the determination to preserve wisdom and ethical conduct.

In Buddhist traditions, Mahākāla is understood as a protector of the Dharma, meaning the teachings of Buddhism. His role is not to create harm, but to prevent obstacles such as ignorance, confusion, and destructive behavior from undermining spiritual practice. While the details of his role vary across schools and regions, he is consistently associated with protection rather than aggression.

Mahākāla is often depicted with a fierce expression, dark coloring, and a powerful stance. These features are symbolic. His dark color represents the absorption of negativity and the vastness of awareness, while his fierce appearance conveys decisiveness and clarity in confronting harmful forces. In Tibetan Buddhism, Mahākāla appears in multiple forms, each associated with specific protective functions and lineages.

Across the regions where Mahākāla is known, he represents the principle that compassion and wisdom sometimes require firmness and resolve. Although artistic styles, rituals, and interpretations differ among cultures, his symbolism consistently points toward protection guided by ethical intention. Mahākāla's presence in Buddhist traditions highlights the importance of guarding what is beneficial while addressing challenges with strength and clarity.

Hayagrīva

Hayagrīva is known as a protective figure associated with the removal of obstacles and harmful influences. He appears primarily in Vajrayana Buddhism, especially in Tibet, Nepal, Mongolia, and Himalayan regions, and has roots in Indian Buddhist traditions. Hayagrīva represents forceful compassion, meaning the use of strength guided by wisdom and ethical intention.

In Buddhist teachings, Hayagrīva is understood as a protector who confronts negative forces that hinder understanding and wellbeing. His role is not associated with anger or violence, but with the decisive removal of ignorance, fear, and destructive patterns. Interpretations of Hayagrīva vary by tradition, yet he is consistently linked with protection, clarity, and transformation.

Hayagrīva is commonly depicted with a fierce expression and a horse's head, which gives him his name. This imagery is symbolic. The horse's head represents powerful energy, alertness, and the ability to overcome stubborn obstacles. In Tibetan Buddhism, Hayagrīva is often associated with protective rituals and meditation practices aimed at strengthening resolve and dispelling harmful influences.

Across the regions where Hayagrīva is known, he represents the principle that compassion can take strong and active forms when needed. Although artistic styles and ritual roles differ among cultures, his symbolism consistently points toward courage, protection, and the transformation of negative forces into clarity and strength. Hayagrīva's presence in Buddhist traditions highlights the role of disciplined power when guided by wisdom and care.

Marīcī

Marīcī is known in Buddhism as a protective deity associated with light, dawn, and visibility. She appears primarily in Mahayana and Vajrayana Buddhism, with important roles in India, Tibet, Nepal, China, and Japan. Marīcī is often connected with the first light of day, symbolizing clarity, awareness, and protection from unseen dangers.

In Buddhist traditions, Marīcī is understood as a guardian figure who offers protection from harm, confusion, and fear. Rather than representing physical combat, her role emphasizes concealment, safe passage, and the ability to move through the world without obstruction. Interpretations of her function vary by region, but she is consistently associated with guidance, alertness, and protective awareness.

Marīcī is commonly depicted riding a chariot, sometimes drawn by animals, and surrounded by rays of light. These images symbolize speed, illumination, and the power of visibility. In East Asian Buddhism, particularly in Japan, Marīcī became associated with protection for travelers and warriors, while in Tibetan traditions she appears in ritual contexts related to safeguarding and clarity.

Across the regions where Marīcī is known, she represents the principle that light reveals and protects. Although artistic forms and ritual practices differ among cultures, her symbolism consistently points toward awareness, preparedness, and the protective quality of clear perception. Marīcī's presence in Buddhist traditions highlights the role of insight and alertness in moving safely through both physical and mental landscapes.

Devas
(Heavenly Beings)

Devas are celestial beings who inhabit higher realms within Buddhist cosmology. They are powerful and long-lived, but not fully awakened and remain subject to change. Devas often appear in Buddhist stories to illustrate impermanence, responsibility, and the limits of power without wisdom.

Indra

Indra is known in Buddhism as a deva, or heavenly being, and is often referred to as Śakra or Śakra Devānām Indra, meaning "King of the Devas." He appears in Buddhist traditions across India, Sri Lanka, Southeast Asia, Tibet, China, Korea, and Japan, where he represents leadership, responsibility, and the exercise of power guided by ethical awareness. Unlike creator gods, Indra in Buddhism is understood as a powerful but impermanent being who remains subject to change and learning.

In Buddhist texts, Indra is frequently portrayed as a supporter and protector of the Buddha and the Buddhist teachings. He is said to rule the Trāyastriṃśa Heaven, a celestial realm where devas enjoy long lives and great comfort. However, Buddhist teachings emphasize that even devas are not fully awakened and remain within the cycle of rebirth. Indra's role highlights that status and power do not replace wisdom and insight.

Indra is commonly depicted as a regal figure, sometimes holding a thunderbolt or shown in armor, symbolizing authority and strength. In Buddhist art and literature, these attributes represent leadership and responsibility rather than domination. In Southeast Asian traditions, Indra appears frequently in temple art and stories, while in East Asian Buddhism he is often shown as a guardian figure who respects and protects the Dharma.

Across the regions where Indra is known, he represents the principle that power carries responsibility and must be guided by ethical conduct. Although his name, imagery, and emphasis vary by culture, his presence in Buddhist traditions reinforces the idea that wisdom and compassion are more important than rank or authority. Indra's role highlights the Buddhist view that all beings, even heavenly ones, continue to learn and grow.

Candra

Candra is known in Buddhism as a deva, or heavenly being, associated with the moon. He appears in Buddhist traditions across India, Sri Lanka, Southeast Asia, Tibet, China, and Japan, often through stories, art, and symbolic references rather than central religious practice. Candra represents calmness, reflection, and the rhythms of time and nature.

In Buddhist teachings, Candra is not a creator or ultimate authority. Like other devas, he is understood as a powerful but impermanent being who exists within the cycle of rebirth. His presence in Buddhist literature often serves to illustrate natural order, balance, and the idea that even celestial beings remain subject to change and learning.

Candra is commonly depicted with lunar symbols, cool coloring, or a serene appearance that reflects the quiet light of the moon. In South and Southeast Asian traditions, he appears in temple art and cosmological descriptions. In East Asian contexts, lunar symbolism is sometimes emphasized more than the individual figure, connecting the moon with mindfulness, impermanence, and calm observation.

Across the regions where Candra is known, he represents the principle that nature itself can be a teacher. The changing phases of the moon reflect impermanence, balance, and continuity. Although cultural expressions vary, Candra's role in Buddhist traditions highlights themes of calm awareness, reflection, and harmony with the natural world.

Specialized Protective Figures

(Buddha Devas)

Buddha Devas are specialized protective figures associated with Buddhist cosmology and symbolism. They are not individual historical beings, but representations of protective forces connected to Buddhist teachings and sacred spaces. They help illustrate how Buddhist traditions understand guardianship and cosmic order.

Dukkar

Dukkar is a protective figure in Buddhism associated with shelter, safety, and the prevention of harm. She is best known in Tibetan and Himalayan Buddhist traditions, where she appears as a guardian who shields beings from obstacles, danger, and negative influences. Dukkar's name is commonly linked to the image of a white parasol or umbrella, a traditional symbol of protection and refuge.

In Buddhist teachings, Dukkar represents protection that is calm and encompassing rather than forceful. Her role emphasizes creating safe conditions in which understanding and compassionate action can develop. While interpretations of her function vary by region and lineage, she is consistently understood as offering protection through awareness, care, and steadiness rather than confrontation.

Dukkar is often depicted holding or crowned by a white umbrella, sometimes with multiple faces or arms. These features symbolize the ability to offer shelter in many directions at once. The white color represents purity, clarity, and openness. In Tibetan Buddhism, Dukkar is associated with practices intended to remove obstacles, protect travelers, and maintain stability in uncertain circumstances.

Across the regions where Dukkar is known, she represents the principle that protection can be gentle yet effective. Although artistic forms and ritual practices differ among cultures, her symbolism consistently points toward refuge, reassurance, and the creation of space for wellbeing. Dukkar's presence in Buddhist traditions highlights the importance of safety and care as foundations for clarity and growth.

Garuḍa

Garuḍa is a mythical being associated with strength, speed, and protection in Buddhist traditions. He appears in Buddhism primarily through Indian, Tibetan, Nepalese, and Himalayan contexts, and is also known in parts of East and Southeast Asia. In Buddhism, Garuḍa is understood not as a creator figure, but as a powerful being who exists within the broader cosmological framework of the Buddhist world.

In Buddhist teachings, Garuḍa is often associated with protection from danger and the overcoming of harmful forces. He is especially linked with stories involving nāgas, or serpent beings, where he represents the ability to confront fear and transform threatening situations. These narratives are understood symbolically, pointing to the overcoming of obstacles, ignorance, or inner conflict rather than literal combat.

Garuḍa is commonly depicted as a large bird-like being or a figure with wings, conveying speed, alertness, and expansive vision. In Tibetan Buddhism, Garuḍa imagery appears in protective contexts and symbolic teachings related to fearlessness and freedom from constraint. In other regions, Garuḍa may appear more often in art and mythological references than in everyday religious practice.

Across the regions where Garuḍa is known in Buddhism, he represents the principle of fearless movement and protection through awareness. Although artistic forms and cultural emphasis vary, his symbolism consistently points toward freedom, vigilance, and the capacity to rise above danger. Garuḍa's presence in Buddhist traditions highlights the role of strength and clarity when guided by ethical intention.

Judges of Karma and Death

These figures are associated with moral consequence, death, and rebirth. Rather than acting as creators or punishers, they symbolize the natural results of actions and the importance of ethical responsibility. Their presence reinforces the Buddhist emphasis on impermanence, accountability, and mindful conduct.

Yama

Yama is known in Buddhism as a figure associated with death, moral consequence, and the passage between lives. He appears in Buddhist traditions across India, Tibet, Nepal, China, Korea, Japan, and Southeast Asia, primarily within teachings about karma and rebirth. In Buddhism, Yama is not a creator or ultimate judge, but a symbolic figure who reflects the workings of cause and effect.

In Buddhist texts, Yama is often described as presiding over judgments that reveal the results of one's actions. These accounts are understood differently across traditions. In many contexts, Yama's role is symbolic, illustrating how actions lead to consequences rather than depicting an external being who punishes or rewards. His presence emphasizes responsibility, ethical awareness, and reflection on one's conduct.

Yama is commonly depicted with a stern or formidable appearance, sometimes holding tools associated with judgment or time. This imagery is not meant to inspire fear, but to convey seriousness and inevitability. In Tibetan Buddhism, Yama is closely linked with teachings on impermanence and the cycle of rebirth, while in East Asian traditions he appears in stories and art that encourage moral reflection and accountability.

Across the regions where Yama is known, he represents the principle that actions matter. Although artistic forms and narrative details vary by culture, his symbolism consistently points toward impermanence, responsibility, and the natural consequences of behavior. Yama's presence in Buddhist traditions highlights the importance of ethical living and mindful awareness of how choices shape experience.

Glossary

Awakening

In Buddhism, awakening refers to deep understanding of reality and freedom from ignorance, confusion, and suffering. It is achieved through wisdom, ethical conduct, and insight.

Bodhisattva

An enlightened being who is dedicated to helping others reduce suffering and gain understanding. Bodhisattvas choose compassion and service over personal liberation alone.

Buddha

A fully awakened being who has attained complete understanding of reality and teaches paths that help others awaken. Buddhism recognizes both historical and symbolic Buddhas.

Buddha Devas

A general term used to describe symbolic or protective heavenly beings associated with Buddhist cosmology. They are not individual historical figures, but represent guardianship and protection within Buddhist traditions.

Compassion

A central Buddhist quality referring to care for the suffering of others and the wish to help reduce that suffering through understanding and ethical action.

Dharma

The teachings of Buddhism, including guidance on understanding suffering, ethical conduct, meditation, and wisdom.

Dharmapāla

A protective figure associated with guarding Buddhist teachings and ethical principles. Their fierce appearance is symbolic, representing strength, clarity, and decisiveness rather than aggression.

Deva

A celestial or heavenly being who inhabits higher realms within Buddhist cosmology. Devas are powerful and long-lived, but not fully awakened and remain subject to change and rebirth.

Impermanence

The Buddhist principle that all things change and nothing remains fixed. Understanding impermanence helps reduce attachment and suffering.

Karma

The principle that actions have consequences. In Buddhism, karma refers to how intentions and actions shape future experiences rather than fate or punishment.

Meditation

A set of practices used in Buddhism to develop awareness, concentration, and insight. Meditation supports understanding of the mind and the nature of experience.

Middle Way

A teaching attributed to Gautama Buddha that emphasizes balance between extremes. It guides ethical living, meditation, and insight.

Pure Land

A concept in some Buddhist traditions describing a realm where conditions support spiritual learning and growth.

Rebirth

The Buddhist teaching that life continues through a cycle of existence shaped by karma. Rebirth does not imply a permanent soul, but continuity of cause and effect.

Suffering

In Buddhism, suffering refers broadly to dissatisfaction, distress, and unease experienced in life. Understanding suffering is the starting point for Buddhist practice.

Transcendent Wisdom

Insight into the true nature of reality, including impermanence and non-attachment. It goes beyond ordinary conceptual thinking.

Vajra

A symbolic object meaning "thunderbolt" or "diamond." It represents indestructible clarity, strength, and awakened awareness.

Vajrayana

A form of Buddhism that developed primarily in the Himalayan regions. It emphasizes symbolic imagery, ritual practices, and meditation focused on transformation.